The Light *of* Forgiveness

THE SACRAMENT OF RECONCILIATION FOR TEENS

Father Paul Farren

PARACLETE PRESS
BREWSTER, MASSACHUSETTS

2015 First printing

The Light of Forgiveness: The Sacrament of Reconciliation for Teens

Copyright © 2015 by Father Paul Farren

ISBN 978-1-61261-758-9

Scripture quotations are taken from from *The Jerusalem Bible* © 1966 by Darton Longman & Todd Ltd and Doubleday and Company Ltd.

The Paraclete Press name and logo (dove on cross) are trademarks of Paraclete Press, Inc.

Library of Congress Cataloging-in-Publication Data
Farren, Paul (Catholic priest)
  The light of forgiveness : the sacrament of reconciliation for teens / Father Paul Farren.
    pages cm
  Includes bibliographical references.
  ISBN 978-1-61261-758-9
  1. Catholic teenagers—Religious life. 2. Absolution. 3. Forgiveness of sin. 4. Forgiveness—Religious aspects—Catholic Church. 5. Reconciliation—Religious aspects—Catholic Church. 6. Sacraments—Religious aspects—Catholic Church. I. Title.
  BX2355.F37 2015
  264'.02086—dc23   2015026375

10 9 8 7 6 5 4 3 2 1

Published by Paraclete Press
Brewster, Massachusetts
www.paracletepress.com

Printed in the United States of America

To my father,
who continues to teach me so much

Contents

Introduction

Discussion about the sacrament of Reconciliation can cause many reactions. People can struggle with it. There can be many misunderstandings. These misunderstandings can lead to fear. In the past, preparation for celebrating the sacrament of Reconciliation was often done in the context of the fear of hell! There is a wonderful short story written by Frank O'Connor, "My First Confession." In the story a young boy, Jackie, tells of how he prepared for and celebrated his First Confession. A lady who was called Miss Ryan prepared him. About her he said,

> Hell had the first place in her heart. She lit
> a candle, took out a new half-crown, and
> offered it to the first boy who would hold one
> finger, only one finger!—in the flame for five
> minutes by the school clock. Being always
> very ambitious I was tempted to volunteer,

> but I thought it might look greedy. Then she
> asked were we afraid of holding one finger—
> only one finger!—in a little candle flame for
> five minutes and not afraid of burning all over
> in roasting hot furnaces for all eternity. "All
> eternity! Just think of that! A whole lifetime
> goes by and it's nothing, not even a drop in
> the ocean of your sufferings."

This certainly was a dramatic way to introduce the sacrament, which we are told is a gift from God!

In this book I want reveal the true meaning of the sacrament and the gift and power it is in our lives. To do this I needed to hear the questions that young people had about the sacrament.

We are blessed in our parish of St. Eugene's Cathedral in the diocese of Derry, Ireland, to have a youth community who live together, pray together, and do school retreats together. It is a sign of the vibrancy of the Church and the reality that people of all ages want to get to know Jesus better and share their faith with others.

I asked them what questions they had about the sacrament of Reconciliation. Their first question was, "Why is Confession so scary?" Obviously fear is still associated with the sacrament. They also asked, "Why is the sacrament so formal?" They wanted to know what one actually had to say in the celebration of the sacrament. They asked about the role of the priest. "What about confessing straight to God?" Throughout the book their questions will pop up, and I will try to answer them.

I will answer them in the bigger context of how we live our lives and what role God desires to have in our lives. It is in this way that the gift and power of the sacrament will become obvious. I firmly believe that the sacrament of Reconciliation is one of the most powerful gifts that we can accept in our lives. The sacrament has the power to transform our lives and make us so full of joy. It can also transform the Church and society. If we really understand and accept the gift of the sacrament of Reconciliation from God, we will be changed.

When Pope Francis was speaking about the sacrament of Reconciliation, he said:

> Confession should not be "torture," but everyone should leave the confessional with happiness in their hearts, with their faces radiating hope, albeit at times—we know—

bathed in the tears of conversion and joy derived from it. It should be a liberating encounter, enriched with humanity, through which one can educate in mercy, which does not exclude but rather includes the just obligation to atone for, to the extent possible, the wrong committed. Thus the faithful will feel called to confess frequently, and will learn to do so in the best of ways, with that gentleness of soul that does so much good for the heart—also the heart of the confessor! In this way we priests enable the personal relationship with God to grow, so that his Kingdom of love and peace expands in hearts.

In the sacrament of Reconciliation we can find happiness and the powerful gift of hope. We are liberated—set free. We are enabled to come closer and closer to God. It is an amazing gift.

Using the Youth Team's questions and other questions, too, this book will uncover some aspects of the amazing gift that the sacrament is. No book could uncover all the aspects of the gift because the gift is as big as the one giving the gift—God!

How do we live our lives?

To enable us to uncover any aspects of a gift from God, we need to look at our own lives, because it is into the reality of our lives that God gives us his gifts. So we need to ask: How do we live our lives? In what context do we live our lives? As people of faith, in what context do we live our faith?

It is impossible to live life in isolation. It simply can't be done. Nobody is independent. We are all dependent on one another. Just take a moment to think about how many people are involved in your life right now. Your family? Your friends? Your teachers? But what about the people who made your clothes? What about those who transported them to the shop? What about those who sold them to you?

What about those who made the money or credit card you used? The list goes on and on. We need each other. These relationships of dependence can be great gifts or sources of abuse. However, in some ways they are the context in which we live our lives. We live our lives in the context of inter-dependent relationships. At times we are willing to acknowledge this reality, and at times we refuse to acknowledge it and we assert our imagined independence! At times like this we declare, "I don't need anybody—I am self-sufficient!" Really?

One problem with our need of others is that we can come to resent that need. We can see needing one another as something negative, and that can make us react to one another negatively. This is where God comes in.

God obviously doesn't see need and dependency as negative. How do we know this? We know it because God chooses need and dependency as ways in which to relate to us. This might sound surprising since God is all-powerful and all-knowing, and yet this is God's choice.

In the book of the prophet Isaiah there is a fascinating passage where God says:

With heaven my throne
and earth my footstool,
what house could you build for me,
what place could you make for my rest?
All of this was made by my hand
and all of this is mine—it is the Lord
   who speaks.
But my eyes are drawn to the person
of humble and contrite spirit
who trembles at my word.

God is telling us that he has everything. He is all-powerful. However, he is drawn to the person of humble and contrite spirit. His desire is to be in friendship—in relationship—with each one of us. You may object and say that doesn't prove that he needs us or is dependent on us. In ways you are right. God doesn't need us and is not dependent on us. However, he chooses to need us and be dependent on us in his relationship with us. He creates this dependency by giving us free will. When God desires to be in relationship with us, he makes himself vulnerable. We don't have to respond to his vulnerability, but the fulfillment of God's desire is dependent on our response. God needs us to respond to enable him to be in relationship with us. God will never force himself into our lives. He waits for us to welcome him into our lives: a beautiful illustration of Divine Humility.

Since God chooses to need us and be dependent on us, he obviously doesn't see either need or dependency as negative but, instead, as beautiful and positive.

Jesus takes this one step further—this relationship of need and dependency that can be so positive and so powerful. When Jesus came into the world he introduced a completely new way of living. He wanted us all to live as brothers and sisters. However, more than that, he wanted us all to live as members of his body. What does that mean?

What does it mean to be the body of Christ? It means that Jesus wants us to be his presence in the world today. He is depending on us. St. Teresa of Avila says,

Christ has no body now but yours—no
hands—no feet on earth but yours.
Yours are the eyes with which he looks with
compassion on this world.
Yours are the feet with which he walks to do good.

Yours are the hands with which he blesses all
    the world.
Yours are the hands—yours are the feet—
yours are the eyes—
you are his Body.
Christ has no body now on earth but yours.

This is the incredible trust and dependence that Jesus has in us. He wants us to allow him to be present through our lives. This can change the whole structure of society.

We live in a society that is structured like a pyramid: a hierarchical shape sloping upward from a massive but relatively powerless base to a narrow top where all the power resides. The journey upward is all about winning and getting to the top. In order to get to the top you have to knock people down because the space as you forge your way to the top gets narrower and narrower. It's all about competition. But if you step out of the pyramid and into Jesus's way of life, you step into a body. There is no room for competition in a body. The hand is not in competition with the foot. The eye is not exerting its superiority over the mouth. For the body to work, competition must be banished, and every part has to do its own unique thing. Competition would kill the body, but cooperation allows it to flourish and grow. When we cooperate and realize we need one another, we live as brothers and sisters. This is the vision of Jesus. Yet we can move far from that vision, and we can do it without even noticing.

We can move very quickly from living a relationship of brothers and sisters to living a relationship of competitiveness. Competition enters into many of the relationships that we have, and it can start at a very early age. I don't know if they still have the dreadful Bonny Baby Show, a competition in which innocent babies are paraded and judged in terms of their looks. It beggars belief.

We often use competition to motivate people. We use competition to increase people's self esteem—if they win! Competition often becomes the way we relate to others. You might go home and tell your parents that you got a B on your test, and your parents might say, "Very good." But then your parents might try to find out what the rest of the class got so they can decide if the B was really good or not! Competition drives so much. It defines so many relationships.

It is a very small step from seeing the other person as a fellow competitor to seeing him as a threat. If that person beats me, I won't get what I want, so that person is a threat to me. The world has a way of making us view others as threats. We saw that in a very literal way with the Swine Flu scare. I don't wish to undermine the real need there is to be careful about spreading disease, but the Swine Flu reaction made everybody a threat to everybody else. Don't touch me, because you could contaminate me! There is a true story about a meeting that happened during the Swine Flu period. The meeting included people with learning disabilities. At the beginning of the meeting an announcement was made that due to the Swine Flu all had to refrain from hugging that morning. At about 12:10 PM a boy with Down's syndrome went around the room hugging people. When he was asked to stop he said, "Why? The morning is over!" We can become threats to one another, threats to one another's position, threats to one another's career path.

It is a very short step to go from seeing the other as a threat to seeing the other as an enemy. Then war breaks out. It is our natural instinct to defend our territory and fight our enemy. In some ways it is a very understandable journey to go from being a brother or a sister to becoming a competitor, to becoming a threat, to becoming an enemy. This journey has nothing to do with God. It has nothing to do with Jesus. It is a journey that Jesus desires us to reject. He never wants us to move away from being each other's brothers and sisters. This is a profound challenge that we have to face to remain brothers and sisters in a world that promotes competition. How do we remain as brothers and sisters? How do we remain as the body of Christ?

This can be difficult. Often it seems easier to be competitors rather than each other's brothers and sisters, dependent on each other. When we are brothers and sisters we relate to each other as equals with beautiful and unique gifts. St. Paul speaks about this very directly in his letter to the Philippians. He says,

There must be no competition among you.

Paul's vision is for us to be united in love with a common purpose and a common mind: to become the body of Christ and to become one with the mind of Jesus. He goes on to say,

> Always consider the other person to be
> better than yourself, so that nobody thinks
> of his own interests first but everybody
> thinks of other people's interests instead. In
> your minds you must be the same as Christ
> Jesus.

This can be difficult. It is about living in holy communion with one another. This is what the Eucharist is about—the Mass. We receive the body of Christ so that we can go out and be the body of Christ. We receive Holy Communion so that we can live in holy communion. That can be tough. Once I realized that very forcefully.

In October 2006 I visited a prison outside Addis Ababa in Ethiopia. It was the most hopeless place I have ever been in. It was simply a field with a few mud huts. In the field there were about 280 young men walking about purposelessly. Their spirits were so broken that they didn't even try to escape. They no longer dreamed of freedom. As part of our visit we were brought into a mud hut that served as their kitchen. It had no light except that coming from the open door. In primitive and less than hygienic conditions, people were baking bread for the prisoners. It was unleavened bread exactly like Holy Communion at Mass, only bigger. The chaplain, who was showing us around, lifted a piece of the bread and broke it and offered me a bit to try. I refused. I refused to share their bread because I could not cope with their circumstances. I could not enter fully into the dreadful reality of their lives. I refused to be in communion with them. Afterward I felt ashamed. I wanted to fix their reality, but I didn't want to stand with them in their reality—united with them as their brother. In many ways that day I sinned. Not eating the bread wasn't a sin, but the attitude it revealed was a sin.

So in what context do we live our lives? We live them in the context of relationships—relationships of dependency and need that can be so positive and so powerful that we are led by them to love itself. In many ways the relationships we live throughout our lives never change, from the moment of our conception to the moment of our death. While we live in the womb we need our mother to nourish us and literally give us a lifeline. Then at the time of death we are completely dependent, too. We are weak and fragile at the beginning and the end of our earthly lives. However, if truth be told, we are weak and fragile throughout all of our lives. Often we try to hide it; often we forbid ourselves to admit it!

Sr. Maria Boulding was a nun in England. She was a very powerful and capable person. However, she suffered from cancer at the end of her life. In the last months of her life she reflected on her illness and her increasing weakness and her increasing need of others. She said:

> These months of illness have become for me a journey of discovery. I have discovered that suffering and happiness are by no means incompatible; on the contrary, my weakness seems to help. New understanding of friendship, love and tenderness has been given. There is a way to walk as I grow weaker. Love is communicated at levels of shared suffering, tenderness and bodily care that I have never touched before, and my weakness has been needed to open them.

The sacramental reality of Christ's body has become tangible. I am being shown the depth of love in those closest to me, and discovering in new ways what Christian community is.
I am able now to accept the love of others, and believe in it, like a helpless child who has nothing to give except its need. Now when I am useless, can do little in the way of work, and cannot make a difference, all I can give is my need of other people.

Our realization that we are weak, that we need others and that we are dependent on others, can give us great freedom and allow us to enter into real friendships. These friendships are not built on our trying to pretend to be other than what we really are. These are real friendships.

This is where God, the Church, and sacraments come in. Friendship is the key. God wants to be in friendship with us. He wants us to positively choose to have him as our friend. He stands at the door of our life and he knocks, but he will never come into our lives himself. He has too much respect for us to do that. He waits until we open the door. When we do open the door, he showers us with gifts. Each gift reveals to us that God loves us. Each gift brings to life the words spoken by God in the book of the prophet Isaiah:

> Do not be afraid, I have redeemed you.
> I have called you by your name; you are
> mine. You are precious in my eyes. You are
> honoured and I love you. Do not be afraid; I
> am with you.

God always wants to calm our fear. He wants us to know that we are precious. He wants us to know that he loves us. We are made in the image and likeness of God, and we are loved. We are loved not for what we do or what we say or anything else. We are loved because we are beautiful and because God marvels at us. If we could only see ourselves as God sees us, we would be so happy.

How does God see me?

It can be difficult to be yourself.
It can be difficult to know yourself. So often we try
to create an image of ourselves that we think will
be acceptable to others. When we do that, we can
move away from the truth of who we are. We pretend to be the person we have constructed, and we
reject who we really are because we feel that who we
really are is simply not good enough, not acceptable
enough, not popular enough.

The musical *Les Misérables* is a powerful story. It is
about a man called Jean Valjean who stole food to
enable his family to survive. He got caught and was
sent to jail for the theft. On his release—because
he was still on parole—if he wanted to work, he
had to produce a certificate that declared his former
convict status. This reality meant that nobody

wanted to employ him. He was reduced to stealing simply to survive. He met a very generous bishop who brought him into his house and fed him. When Jean Valjean was leaving, he stole some silver from the house. He was caught by the police and brought back to face the bishop. Valjean had told the police that the bishop had given the silver to him as a gift. The bishop corroborated his story and also presented him a beautiful pair of candlesticks. Profoundly moved by the saintly bishop's kindness and compassion, Valjean made a decision there and then to transform his life. He adopted a new identity and became a very successful businessman under this new identity. Ultimately he became mayor of his town. One dogged policeman persisted in looking for him because he had broken his parole, but was unable to find him.

One day in the town a runaway cart struck a man and pinned him underneath. Valjean, a man of great physical strength, managed to lift the cart and free the man. The dogged policeman recognized the former convict from his strength, but Valjean escaped into the crowd. Another man was arrested and wrongly charged.

This left Jean Valjean with a terrible dilemma. If he said nothing, an innocent man was going to be condemned. If he admitted who he was, he himself was going to be condemned. His dilemma is powerfully captured in the song "Who Am I?"

During the trial of the innocent man Jean Valjean realized he could no longer live a lie. He could not deny who he was. He had to be true to himself and to God. In a moment of high drama, he rips open his shirt and reveals his prison number and declares his name.

Jean Valjean's agonizing questions are ones we all ask: Do I dare let others see who I am? What about God?—does he see me as I really am, and does he love me anyway?

These can be scary questions because sometimes we can really struggle with the reality of who we are, and we hide from that reality in every possible way. This is understandable, because there can be such pressure placed on us today to fit into society. At one level we are led to believe that we are living in the most liberal and free time in history. The impression is that nobody conforms and everybody just does what they want. Is this the truth? Does the evidence back this up? Perhaps not! In the Western world we seem to be living in a time of profound conformity. Being slaves to fashion is an international phenomenon. If a couple of famous people get tattoos, a craze for tattoos takes over. If a couple of famous men grow beards, facial hair is everywhere! Why do so many people wear skinny jeans nowadays? It is certainly not because they suit everybody! There is such a drive for conformity today at so many levels that our individuality and uniqueness can be much diluted. We can see them as negatives as we desperately try to "be like" rather than "stand out"!

So who am I and how does God see me? God sees me as outstanding. I am outstanding! There is a beautiful book in the Bible—the Song of Songs. It is a powerful and dynamic love story full of action and drama. The lover is pursuing the beloved.

> How beautiful you are, my love, how
> beautiful you are!

Who am I and how does God see me? I am beautiful, and God sees me as beautiful. Nothing or nobody can ever take that reality away from me. I am beautiful, and God is in love with me. But God is a shy pursuer. In the Song of Songs, God's shyness is obvious.

> See where he stands behind the wall. He looks in at the window, he peers through the lattice.

It is like that shyness that somebody can have when they are in love. We are told that God comes leaping over the mountains and bounding over the hills like a young gazelle—but then God stops. It is as if you are running to the person you love, but when you get close to them you lose your nerve. God waits behind the wall. It is as if God's nerve has faltered! Then God peers in at the window, and then God calls. God invites. Our God says:

> Come then, my love,
> my lovely one, come.
> My dove, hiding in the clefts of the rock,
> in the coverts of the cliff,
> show me your face,
> let me hear your voice;
> for your voice is sweet
> and your face is beautiful.

God finds his nerve; but maybe we have lost our nerve? Then with beautiful and gentle words God calls us. God calls us because the love that God has for us is beyond anything we can imagine. It is a love that

> no flood can quench,
> no torrents drown.

When we respond to this passionate, life-giving love that God has for us, we will stay forever young. We will have real energy and life in our relationship with God. We are able to say with the bride in the Song of Songs,

> Draw me in your footsteps. Let us run.

We can run in the footsteps of God when we are confident in God's love for us and in our own beauty. We can run in those footsteps when we know who we are and how God sees us—God's beloved. Each one of us is uniquely beautiful. Imagine a field full of golden daffodils. In the middle of the daffodils is one red tulip! How do you react? Do you look at the red tulip and say, "Poor, deformed daffodil"? Or do you look at the tulip and say, "What a beautiful tulip in the middle of all those daffodils"? Can we accept that we are beautiful in our uniqueness?

Truthfully many of us can struggle at times to believe and accept this. We can struggle to believe that we really are beautiful. Sometimes, like Jean Valjean, we may want to leave what we consider our old self behind. We may struggle to accept who we are. This struggle can come when we have a very limited understanding of beauty. How would you define beauty? Was Jean Valjean, the mayor and the successful businessman, beautiful? Was Valjean, the prisoner, beautiful? Is it what we do or how we look that makes us beautiful? You would be forgiven for answering yes to this question. But our understanding of beauty is essentially superficial.

We get evidence of this from the vast numbers of people who are having cosmetic surgery. Who decides that the natural aging process is not beautiful to look at? Our definition of beauty seems to be so narrow as to be ridiculous. How often in the morning do you stand in front of the mirror and say, "Thank you, God, for making me, and making me beautiful"? It can be a very difficult thing to do.

Maybe sometimes we stand in front of the mirror and say, "What am I going to do with that?" Yet the only definition of beauty that really matters is God's definition, and God sees each one of us as beautiful. God sees beauty in every aspect of our being. Quite simply, God sees us as completely beautiful. He has made us in his own image and likeness. He has given us the gift of life, and we are beautiful; so we can stand in front of the mirror every day and thank God for what we see.

Where is God in my life?

The truth of our beauty lies in the fact that God has created us and God makes no mistakes. It is from the very core of our being—from the center of our lives—that our beauty comes. Our beauty comes not from the outside but from the inside. What is at the center of our lives? The quick and simple answer to this question is God! God is at the center of our lives. What does that actually mean? What does it mean to say that God is at the center of my life? The Church helps us to answer this question. The Church calls the center of our lives our conscience. Maybe it could be described as the Mission Control of our lives! It is the place we need to go when we have to make decisions. It is the place in our lives where we get the power to do good deeds. In one

of the documents of the Second Vatican Council we
are told,

> Conscience is the most secret core and
> sanctuary of a person. There he is alone with
> God, whose voice echoes in his depths.

Our conscience then is the center of our lives
where God lives. It is amazing to realize that God
lives in each one of us. We don't have to go anywhere to meet God. In our conscience we are united
with God. There is no difference there between how
we see ourselves and how God sees us. In that place
God's ways and God's opinions are our ways and our
opinions. It is the happiest place in our lives because
there we see ourselves as God sees us. Etty Hillesum,
who perished at Auschwitz, was describing perhaps
the place of conscience, the center of her life, when
she said,

> I regained contact with myself, with the
> deepest and best in me, which I call God.

It is an amazing reality that God trusts us so much
that he lives in us. When we find God in our lives,

we find everything that is best in us. When we make the journey into our conscience, we are united and at peace with God. Our conscience, then, is a sacred place in our lives.

The Irish writer Walter Macken describes our conscience like this:

> The inside of you is like a well, a deep well about which you know very little. That must be your soul, where all the real things take place. And if it is a right deep place, and has been tended by your head, then he supposed that God would be deep down in there whispering to you always about the realities, so that would be the real fair land, deep down in yourself.

This is a wonderful image. The center of our lives, our conscience, is "a real fair land." A place of beauty. A place of life. A place of energy and new growth. The place where we are united with God. In our conscience there is no distance between us and God. There we share fully in God's life. When we make the journey into our conscience, we discover how God wants us to live our lives. Then we must live our lives that way to be true to ourselves. To do anything else would be wrong. That is why Blessed John Henry Newman could say,

> Certainly, if I am obliged to bring religion into after-dinner toasts (which indeed does not seem quite the thing), I shall drink—to the Pope, if you please—still, to Conscience first, and to the Pope afterwards.

Newman was clearly stating that nothing comes between us and God—not even the pope! The Church teaches this very clearly, too, when it states:

> Man has the right to act in conscience and in freedom so as personally to make moral decisions. He must not be forced to act contrary to his conscience. Nor must he be prevented from acting according to his conscience, especially in religious matters.

This highlights the need for freedom of conscience to be respected. We need to be able to act according to our conscience. However, that does not mean that we just do what we want. It doesn't mean that whatever feels good for me is what I should do. This is one of the problems in the world today. People make decisions without any reference to anything or anybody. Often that type of attitude can reveal a disconnect from the center of our lives—a disconnect from our conscience. When we are in that place in our lives where we are at one with God, we realize that we want what God wants. It is not about what I want. It is about wanting what God wants.

How do we know what God wants?

How do we know what God wants?

How do we make the journey down into the "fair land" of our conscience? We know what God wants when we get to know Jesus. We get to know Jesus when we listen to the Gospel and to the teaching of the Church. We get to know Jesus when we care for those who are poor. We get to know Jesus when we live our lives as active members of his body—the Church. We get to know Jesus when we talk to him and listen to him in prayer.

This is what happened to the apostles. They got to know Jesus so well that when the Holy Spirit came they could go out and proclaim, not their own opinions and thoughts, but the truth of Jesus. The apostles show us how to be powered from the center of our lives. They also show us how not to be! When we speak about sin we will explore that.

After Pentecost the apostles spoke the language of Jesus to everyone, and everyone understood. It was remarkable. What mattered to the apostles was to tell everybody about Jesus. Their focus was Jesus. This can be hard to understand today. We live in a time when we are told that our focus should be ourselves. It is Generation Me! It is all about Me! However, if we make that journey into the "fair land" of our lives, to our conscience, we realize that it is not Generation Me. It is Generation God! I met a man recently who seems to know this and who lives Generation God.

David Alton is a remarkable man. He is a politician in England. He left his party because he did not agree with their stance on abortion. He is now an independent member of the House of Lords. It is very obvious from listening to him and seeing the issues that he tackles as a politician that he allows his policies and his opinions to be shaped by his faith. His relationship with God shapes how he works.

Allowing your friendship with Jesus, alive in the Church, to guide your thoughts and your opinions doesn't seem to be very popular today. It is often seen as weakness—the action of people who can't think for themselves. Today it appears that many baptized people make decisions and take up positions and engage in actions without any reference to Jesus or to his teaching. They have not gone to the center of their lives where they are at one with Jesus. When this happens, their relationship with Jesus fractures—is broken. A broken relationship with Jesus does not bring peace, and sometimes, in an effort to find peace in their broken relationship with Jesus, people delude themselves into a conviction that Jesus must agree with the positions they have adopted. At the very least, they stoutly claim, Jesus must understand that the stance they have taken was taken out of compassion—and what can be wrong with that? Now *compassion* is a beautiful word that conveys both love and pity for the suffering of others. Sadly, today, the word *compassion* is often displaced, wrongly used by people who, in its name, condone actions that can be described as selfish and detrimental to others: actions that do not follow the way of Jesus.

It is remarkable that when the apostles went out after Pentecost they went out with one purpose and one purpose only, and that was to proclaim Jesus.

They were able to proclaim Jesus convincingly because there was no difference between their opinions and his opinions. They believed in Jesus, and they believed in what he said and in what he taught. They desired and they allowed the Holy Spirit to live in their lives and to be active in their lives.

When we welcome the Holy Spirit into our lives, and we give the Spirit freedom in our lives, we live more and more out of the center of our lives—that sacred sanctuary. Then we become more and more the presence of Jesus in the world. When that happens, our focus is no longer ourselves. Our focus is Jesus.

When we allow the Spirit of God to take hold of us, we forget about ourselves; all that matters is Jesus. When all that matters is Jesus, we will bear witness to the truth. Then when we have decisions to make we will return to the Gospel and to the teachings of the Church to find out what Jesus wants us to do. We will do this, not because we are weak and can't make up our own minds, but because we are strong and courageous and we believe that the way of Jesus is the right way.

It is not about persuading myself that Jesus agrees with my actions, or my stances, or my opinions; it is about me walking in the footsteps of Jesus, agreeing with and understanding Jesus, knowing that Jesus is right and knowing that the life I am living is the life his Father wants me to live.

What happens when we don't do what God wants?

It is one thing to know what God wants. It is a completely different thing to do what God wants! We may know the teaching of Jesus. We may know the teaching of the Church, but we may choose not to listen to that teaching. In other words, we may decide not to make the journey to our conscience and may simply follow others, follow the crowd, and give in to temptation. Sometimes we choose to do what we know is wrong. What happens then is that we sin. And what is sin?

Sin is not necessarily when we break a law. This can shock some people who assume that sin is always about breaking of law. It is important that we don't break the law—whether the law of God or the ethical law of the land. However, sin is about much more than breaking a law. We may have different attitudes to laws. We may agree with some and disagree with others. We may think that it is okay to break a law as long as we don't get caught—such as breaking the speed limit when we are driving! But sin is more than this.

To have some notion about what sin is, we need to look at Peter in the Gospels. Peter was the apostle whom Jesus chose to be the rock on which he was going to build his Church. However, in many ways Peter was a disaster! He got many things wrong. He disagreed with Jesus when Jesus told the apostles that he was going to suffer. Jesus reacted to this strongly by saying,

Get behind me, Satan!

When Jesus invited Peter to walk on the water to meet him, Peter jumped in enthusiastically, but then his faith failed him and he began to sink. At the Last Supper Jesus did an outrageous thing as the apostles' Master and host. When they had finished eating, he got up, took off his outer clothes, got down on his knees, and began to wash their feet. This was the action of a slave, not a Master. Peter objected. He was always getting it wrong!

Another time he declared that he, Peter, would give his life for Jesus and was shocked when Jesus responded by telling him that instead Peter would deny him three times. This was the ultimate in getting it wrong. At the most vulnerable time for Jesus—when he was arrested and knew the suffering and death that lay ahead of him—what did Peter do? He said he didn't know him. He denied him. He denied him three times. He rejected Jesus at his hour of greatest need. It was an awful thing to do. When Peter realized what he had done, his reaction was to weep bitterly. Now did Peter weep bitterly because he had broken a law? No, he didn't. Peter wept bitterly because he had denied his friend. This is the heart of sin. Sin is when you deny your friend. Sin is when you reject the one who loves you. That should cause any one of us to be sad—maybe to be heartbroken and, like Peter, to weep bitterly. When we sin, it may involve breaking laws, but the primary thing that happens when we sin is that we do something negative in our friendship with Jesus. When we sin, we hurt our friend. It is as simple and as painful as that.

How do we know what is sinful and what is not? How do we know what hurts Jesus and what doesn't? Put simply, how do we know what is right and what is wrong? These are big questions! We are often led to believe that right and wrong depend on ourselves. If I think it is right, then it is right, and if I think it is wrong, then it is wrong! The Church is often criticized today for telling people what is right and wrong. It is accused of being negative. It may be perceived as being anti-joy! It always seems to tell us what we cannot do. We react to this and defend ourselves by insisting that we are free to do what we want. We might go further and say we have the right to do what we want and that nobody has the right to tell us what we can and cannot do.

Is Jesus anti-joy? Is God negative? Does the Church simply tell us what we cannot do? Does God ignore our right to be free?

No! No! No! No! God respects our freedom so much that he will never push himself into our lives. God is the humble God who pursues us because we are beautiful and he loves us. In the last book of the

Bible, the book of Revelation, we see where God is in our lives. God says,

> I stand at the door and knock. If anyone
> hears me and answers the door I will come
> in and have a meal with that person.

God will never force himself into our lives. He knocks, he calls, and he waits, but he will never open the door himself. We are the ones with the power to open the door or not. If we choose to open the door, we don't open the door to negativity; we don't open the door to a series of "thou shalt nots"! We open the door to life. Jesus tells us,

> I have come so that you may have life and
> have it to the full.

Jesus is not anti-joy. The first place to which he brought the apostles was to a wedding feast! There he changed water into wine. He didn't bring them to "Apostle School" or to a seminary. He brought them to a party! So where does the perception that it is all negative come from? Perhaps the source of the perception could be the Ten Commandments. They sound so negative: full of "thou shalt nots." But are the Ten Commandments negative? They are written in the negative, but are they actually negative? Is God simply trying to curtail our freedom?

Perhaps the truth is quite the opposite. Perhaps the Ten Commandments are a road map to freedom. Could this be possible? If we live by the Ten Commandments, are we curtailed or are we free? Let us look at them and see:

1. I am the Lord your God: you shall not have strange Gods before me.

   When God says we are to have no other gods but him, we are freed from being enslaved by anybody or anything in this world. God doesn't make us into slaves. When God is our God, we realize that he trusts us—he trusts us with free will, he trusts us with his creation, he trusts us with his life when he gives us Jesus in Holy Communion.

2. You shall not take the name of the Lord your God in vain.

   When we respect God and when we respect the name of God, we are freed from arrogance and the belief that we have no need for God—freed from the notion that we are powerful enough on our own.

3. Remember to keep holy the Sabbath Day.
When we keep holy the Sabbath day and rest, we are freed from the notion that we own God's creation, that it is ours to exploit and that this world is all that there is to satisfy us.

4. Honor your father and your mother.
When we honor our father and our mother, we are freed from the fallacy that we know everything and have nothing to learn from those who are older and wiser.

5. You shall not kill.
When we don't kill, we are freed from the horrific repercussions of violence and unnatural death.

6. You shall not commit adultery.
When we don't commit adultery, we are freed from the terrible damage that unfaithfulness in marriage brings.

7. You shall not steal.

8. You shall not bear false witness against your neighbor.

   When we don't steal and when we don't tell lies about others, we are freed from the confusion and destruction that dishonesty always brings.

9. You shall not covet your neighbor's wife.

10. You shall not covet your neighbor's goods.

    When we don't secretly desire that which belongs to another—possessions, husband, wife—we are freed from greed and jealousy.

So, yes, the Ten Commandments sound negative; however, keeping the commandments is far from negative. It is the most positive thing that any one of us can do. It is positive because it allows us to be free, and when we are free, we are joyful.

To be free we need to make right choices. To be free we need to do what is right. The Ten Commandments, as well as being a road map to freedom, are also proof that right and wrong exist. It is wrong for one to be unfaithful in marriage even if one is lonely in that marriage and attracted to another person. Right and wrong exist independently of my personal views.

My nephew Eoghan taught me a lot about right and wrong when he was about two years old. It was not that he was different from any other two-year-old. It is simply because he was a two-year-old. Two-year-olds have simple lives. If they love you, they show it. If they don't love you, they show it. If they want to do what you ask them to do, then they do it. If they don't want to do what you ask them to do, they throw a tantrum. You know where you stand with a two-year-old. You may not always like where you are standing, but at least you are in no doubt about where it is that you stand.

One thing that fascinated me about my nephew was his ability to know right from wrong. People sometimes say to me that children are too young at the age of seven or eight to make their First Confession because at that age they should not be expected to know the difference between right and wrong. Yet when my nephew was two, he knew the difference, and it was obvious that he knew the difference. He'd look around to see who was watching, and then he'd hit his sister or throw his food or break the jigsaw puzzle or whatever. He loved to walk through something his sister or brother had created and wreak havoc and destruction. He knew it was wrong. His awareness of right and wrong was so highly developed that sometimes he would say, "Sorry!" before he hit his sister!

At two Eoghan knew what was right and wrong. At forty-two, if I am honest, sometimes I struggle to know what is right and what is wrong. What happens in between? I think to answer that question we can look at the temptation of Jesus in the desert by the devil. We know that Jesus did not give in to the devil's temptation. He stood firm against the devil. He said, "No!" In fairness he had plenty of reasons to give in to the temptation. He could have said, "I was out in the wilderness on my own for forty days with nobody to talk to or advise me. What else could I do?" However, he chose not to do this. He chose to be consistent. He chose to be faithful. He could make that choice because he was an adult. He believed in the mission that God had sent him to carry out, and nothing was going to distract him from that mission. With Jesus, you always know where you stand.

Temptation is a very powerful force in all our lives. Sadly, the strongest temptation always urges us to do what is wrong. When we give in to temptation—and let's be honest, we all give into temptation sometimes—we subtly try to blur the lines between what is right and what is wrong. We can make excuses for doing what is wrong and even try to convince ourselves and others that what we have done is actually right. For example, we are grumpy at home, and we offer as an excuse that we are under pressure at school. We may well be under pressure at school, but that does not make it right to be grumpy at home. Adults who are unfaithful in marriage may say that they don't feel loved at home. It can be lonely to feel unloved, but that loneliness does not make it right to be unfaithful. We don't share our time or our material possessions with those who are in need on the grounds that we are afraid that we won't have enough for ourselves. Our time and our possessions may be precious to us, but that does not make it right to turn our back on those in need. We may argue that our lives are ours to do with what we want. Yes, the gift of freedom is a great gift, but that does not make it right for us to use it to disrespect or abuse ourselves or others.

Eoghan knew when he was doing what was wrong, and he offered no excuse for it. As we grow older, we learn to make excuses for our wrongdoing and we blur the lines between right and wrong. We try to make right and wrong subjective rather than objective in an effort to justify what we know down there in the fair land of our conscience to be wrong.

When do we do wrong?

We do what is wrong when we sin!
We do what is wrong when we hurt Jesus. We do what is wrong when we don't make the journey down into our conscience where God is. We do wrong when we damage our friendship with him.

I have a theory! I believe that just as there are the two great commandments of love, there are two great sins as well. When the Pharisees asked Jesus,

> Master, which is the greatest commandment of the Law?

Jesus answered,

> You must love the Lord your God with all
> your heart, with all your soul, and with all
> your mind. This is the greatest and the first
> commandment. The second resembles it:
> You must love your neighbour as yourself.

This was such a positive answer from Jesus. The command is to love. It is to love God, to love our neighbor, and to love ourselves. In other words, it is to know God and so fall in love with God. It is to see our neighbor and ourselves as God sees us. These are the commandments, so what are the sins?

The sins are what I describe as the sin of Adam and Eve and the sin of the Innkeeper, and I think that they are the opposite to the great commandments of love. I think that all the sins we know and we commit fit into the two great sins.

So what is the sin of Adam and Eve? The sin of Adam and Eve is the sin of believing you are God. Adam and Eve had everything. They had a loving and creative relationship with God. They had a loving relationship with each other. They were given the gift of the garden of creation. It was a wonderful garden full of life, full of color, full of everything. There was just the one tree that God asked them not to eat from—the tree of knowledge. You know the story. The serpent tempted them. How did the serpent tempt them? What did the serpent say? The serpent said,

> On the day you eat it your eyes will be
> opened and you will be like gods.

It wasn't enough to be children of God. The attraction was to be God himself. I remember seeing a slogan in a shop window in London: "When everything is not enough!" It wasn't enough for Adam and Eve to be who they were. They wanted to be God. They wanted to be God in their own lives so they ate of the tree. Were they fulfilled when they ate from the tree? They were not. When God came looking for them, we have the amazing confession from Adam,

> I was afraid because I was naked, so I hid.

In the desire to be God, rather than feeling all-powerful, Adam realized the truth that he was naked, and he was afraid, so he hid. This reveals that we cannot be independent. We cannot be all-powerful in our lives. We need each other and we need God.

When we commit the sin of attempting to be God, we are unaware of our real need to be a child of God. We act as if we are masters of our own destiny. We believe that we can do what we want and are accountable to nobody. When we play god in our own lives, we treat ourselves with total disrespect and we treat all of God's creation with disrespect. We think we own everything as our right. It is very hard to be my own god and to have any gratitude.

I remember talking to a man called Ronan. Ronan was a young man who had been married for a number of years. He and his wife Joanne were unable to have any children. They decided to adopt two children. They adopted a brother and sister from Central America. When Ronan was talking about his children, he made a most beautiful comment. He said,

> I thank God every day for allowing me to
> meet these beautiful children.

It was a wonderful attitude to have—to be so grateful for having met his children. He didn't own them. He recognized them as a gift. All we have is gift. We actually own nothing. Maybe we have a right to nothing. What do I mean by that?

We live in a time when people are very conscious of their rights. Rights are good, and rights respect boundaries. Rights can allow a person to flourish in ways that are good. Obviously it is a great shame on the world that not every human being has fundamental human rights. It is an utter shame on the world that not everybody has the basic human right to life itself from the moment of conception to natural death. However, I would caution that if all our focus and attention are only on our rights, we can lose sight of the fact that all is gift.

When we realize that all is gift, our attitude to life and all that is in life changes dramatically. If all is gift, then nothing is our right. We don't have a right to a gift. By its very nature the rights pertaining to a gift belong to the giver, not the one who receives. If I give you a gift, you don't have a right to it. It is my choice to give it to you. If you had a right to what I was giving you, then it would not be a gift; it would be an entitlement.

Not one of us is entitled to life itself. The life that each one of us lives is a gift. That gift of life comes from God. God is the giver of the gift of life. It is his free choice that we live. Therefore none of us is

WHEN DO WE DO WRONG? | 59

entitled to be alive. We are gifted with life. When we see our lives as a gift, this changes how we relate to the world, and it puts our rights into perspective. More importantly, it also reveals that we are not the god of our lives. It damages our relationship with God when we behave as if we are the god in our lives. All is gift. All is gift from God. When we love God, as Jesus invites us to, we become more aware that all is gift, and so our primary prayer needs always to be a prayer of thanksgiving. There can be no such thing as thanksgiving in our lives when we believe that we are God.

Our relationship with Jesus changes when we see everything as gift. Our relationship with ourselves changes, too. When we grow in a realization that we are a gift, we naturally become more respectful of ourselves. We care more for ourselves and for our bodies. We treat ourselves much more gently. Our attitude toward others changes as well. This introduces the second great sin—the sin of the Innkeeper in Bethlehem.

What was the sin of the Innkeeper in Bethlehem? Some people think that I am too harsh on the poor Innkeeper on that first Christmas night. This man was doing a roaring trade. His business was booming. There were so many visitors in Bethlehem that night, all there for the census. There must have been a real festival atmosphere—people who hadn't met for a long time greeting each other. Everybody was out on the town. There probably wasn't a free room in the whole of Bethlehem. The inn was full. All the bedrooms were booked. There must have been great activity in the bar. There probably was singing, and if there was space, there might have been some dancing, too. The Innkeeper must have been delighted. He also must have been very busy making sure everybody had enough drink and that everybody was happy.

Then a man came to the door. He was in a difficult position. His wife was in labor, and they had nowhere to stay. The man, Joseph, needed help. The Innkeeper said he had no space for Joseph and his wife. Some people think this was understandable. The inn was booked out. It is not fair to expect the innkeeper to do anything more. I disagree!

Let us picture the scene: there is a woman on a donkey who is in labor. At a time like that you would make space. This is a crisis. Yet the Innkeeper was too busy. Business was probably too good for him to stop. He refused to help. He sent Mary and Joseph and their baby who was about to be born on their way. What sin did he commit? He didn't make space for Jesus. That was his sin. To love our neighbor is to make space for Jesus. When we don't make space for Jesus, we break the second great commandment of love.

You can argue and say that he didn't know it was Jesus. He didn't know he was the Son of God. I would respond by saying he did know it was a person in need. It must have been obvious that Mary was in great need at that time. He did not make space.

This is where the mission of our lives is revealed. God entrusts us with the life of his Son. Jesus tells us,

Whatever you do to the least you do to me.

For me this is the most challenging line in the whole Bible. Sometimes I wish it was deleted! "Whatever you do to the least you do to me." In many ways it is easy to have a relationship with

Jesus in prayer. It is much more difficult to have a relationship with Jesus alive in other people. Yet the call of the second great commandment of love is to make space for Jesus in our lives. Even when it is hard to recognize him, we still need to make space for him. This can be difficult. When we do this, we leave the pyramid model of society. We share the bread of those who are poor. We live in communion with them. We live as the body of Jesus.

St. Paul speaks very powerfully about the body of Jesus. He says,

> Just as the human body, though it is made up of many parts, is a single unit because all these parts, though many, make one body, so it is with Christ. In the one Spirit we were all baptised, Jews as well as Greeks, slaves as well as citizens, and one Spirit was given to us all to drink.
>
> Nor is the body to be identified with any one of its many parts. If the foot were to say, 'I am not a hand and so I do not belong to the body', would that mean that it stopped being part of the body? If the ear were to say, 'I am not an eye, and so I do not belong

to the body', would that mean that it was not
a part of the body? If your whole body was
just one eye, how would you hear anything?
If it was just one ear, how would you smell
anything?

Instead of that, God put all the separate
parts into the body on purpose. If all the
parts were the same, how could it be a
body? As it is, the parts are many but the
body is one. The eye cannot say to the hand,
'I do not need you', nor can the head say to
the feet, 'I do not need you'.

Since we are all different and uniquely beautiful, we
come together in our difference to be the body of
Jesus. St. Paul goes on to tell us very clearly how we
are to treat the body—especially the weakest parts
of the body.

What is more, it is precisely the parts of the
body that seem to be the weakest that are
the indispensable ones; and it is the least
honourable parts of the body that we clothe
with the greatest care. So our more improper
parts get decorated in a way that our more
proper parts do not need. God has arranged
the body so that more dignity is given to the
parts which are without it, and so that there

> may not be disagreements inside the body,
> but that each part may be equally concerned
> for all the others. If one part is hurt, all parts
> are hurt with it. If one part is given special
> honour, all parts enjoy it.

We are to treat the weakest parts of our body with the greatest care and tenderness. When we don't do this, we commit the sin of the Innkeeper. When we do keep the commandment of love, we are blessed. Jesus tells us in the Gospel of St. Luke,

> When you give a lunch or a dinner, do not
> ask your friends, brothers, relations or rich
> neighbours, for fear they repay your courtesy
> by inviting you in return. No; when you have
> a party, invite the poor, the crippled, the
> lame, the blind; that they cannot pay you
> back means that you are blessed.

It is remarkable that Jesus doesn't say that the poor and crippled, blind and lame, will be blessed to have been to your dinner. No, he says you will be blessed for being in their presence.

I witnessed a beautiful mime of this Gospel in St. Martin in the Fields Church in Trafalgar Square in London. The occasion was the presentation of the

Templeton Prize to Jean Vanier. Jean Vanier is the founder of the L'Arche community, a community where people with learning disabilities and their assistants live together as family. They work together and they pray together. Jean began the community over fifty years ago when he brought two men from a "mental asylum" to live with him. It was as simple as that. From that beginning a marvelous community of love and difference and joy and tenderness was born. At the end of the formal presentation of the Templeton Prize to Jean and when all the speeches were over, a table was brought out to the front of the sanctuary. Jean, with the Episcopalian bishop of London, a Catholic bishop, and a few others, set the table. Then they went through the congregation and invited people with learning disabilities to join them at the party. This was done while the song "I Come like a Beggar" was being sung. They all went up around the table and they raised glasses and they pretended to eat and they danced. It was a wonderful moment of joy. In the midst of all the formality, there was great fun, and those of us not invited to the table received a blessing, too, just by being in the presence of those the world sees as weak, poor, and disabled.

The Innkeeper on that first Christmas night missed a blessing by not having the Son of God born in his house. Think about the joy that it would have brought to that house—having a weak, poor, and vulnerable baby born in their midst.

When we stay in the pyramid model of society, we miss out on joy because it is a lonely and competitive journey to the top. When you get there, you are all alone and the only option is to fall down. I heard somebody once say that life is a rat race and the requirement to win the rat race is that you become a rat!

In the summer of 1992 I went to Trosly, a small town north of Paris, to work in the L'Arche community. Trosly is the small village where Jean Vanier bought the house in which he was to live with the two men he had brought from the asylum. I went with noble intentions to help the handicapped. Embedded in a pyramid model of society, I was going to Trosly to help those "poor people." I saw them as people with problems to which I had the solutions! I went not realizing how limited my French was.

The first morning I was there, I was asked if I had a strong back, and I proudly declared that my back was wonderful. Then I was told that I was going to work in the garden. My idea of a garden was a nice flower garden at the front of the house. Their idea of a garden was what could only be described as a vegetable farm. So the first day I was presented with a pair of rubber boots and told that I was a team leader. There would be six people with learning disabilities in my team. We were sent to plant zucchini. Now I didn't even know what zucchini were, let alone how to plant them! So there I was standing with a group of six people with learning disabilities and I was supposed to direct them in carrying out this task. The task itself was beyond me, and, anyway, I didn't know enough French to communicate with them. So I smiled and nodded, and they began their work—and I copied them. It was the moment when I fell out of the pyramid. I wasn't above these men. I was poorer than they were. The question I asked myself that day was, "Who, in truth, is the disabled one here?"

When we realize that every single one of us has abilities and disabilities—when we admit that we all have needs and that we all need each other—it can become easier to live as the body of Christ. It can be easier to love our neighbor as ourselves. It can be easier to make space for Jesus rather than commit the sin of the Innkeeper. But what happens when we do sin? What happens when we behave as if we are God and when we make no space for Jesus in our lives? How does God react when we hurt him? How does God react when we sin?

How does God react when we sin?

Another big question to be answered! What is God's reaction when we sin? What is God's reaction when we reject his friendship—when we refuse to make the journey down into the core of our being where he is whispering to us?

God would be forgiven for washing his hands of us if we persist in our sin. It would be very understandable if God gave up on us. It would be fair if he abandoned us. However, we know that this is not what happens. We hear again his words in the book of the prophet Isaiah:

> Do not be afraid. I have redeemed you. I have called you by your name. You are mine.

He also says in the book of the prophet Isaiah:

> Does a woman forget her baby at the breast,
> or fail to cherish the child of her womb? Yet
> even if these forget, I will never forget you.
> See, I have carved you on the palm of my
> hand.

So it is obvious that when we sin God does not abandon us. It is not possible to remove a carving from the palm of your hand! God is completely committed to us. He never gives up on us. So what does he do? How does God react?

Even if his reaction is not to abandon us when we sin, he would surely be forgiven for punishing us in some other way. In the past when sin was talked about, punishment was also included. The ultimate punishment was to be sent to hell. Yet sending people to hell would seem to be the same as abandoning someone. But God doesn't abandon us, so what, then, is hell?

The *Catechism* answers this question by stating:

> This state of definitive self-exclusion from
> communion with God and the blessed is
> called 'hell'.

The important qualifying word in that statement is "self-exclusion." We make the decision; we do the excluding. This reveals that God trusts us to make up our own minds. He doesn't force himself into our lives. Remember, he stands at the door and knocks. If we choose not be in friendship with God, he will never force friendship on us. He will respect our choice even if it saddens him. He will not insist that we live with him for eternity. In other words, if we don't want to go to heaven, God won't make us go. However, we have to go somewhere. Hell is the place where God is not present. God does not want any of us to go to hell. He wants us to be with him as parents want their children to be with them. It is not God's desire to punish us or condemn us. In fact, he does neither.

In John's Gospel Jesus says:

> For God sent his Son into the world not to condemn the world, but so that through him the world might be saved. No one who believes in him will be condemned; but whoever refuses to believe is condemned already, because he refused to believe in the name of God's only Son. On these grounds

is sentence pronounced: that though the light
has come in to the world men have shown
they prefer darkness to the light because
their deeds were evil.

God does not judge us. He loves us. It is our own actions that judge us. If we say that we want to be with God, our actions need to reveal our choice. We need to allow God to be God in our lives, and we need to make space for Jesus in our lives. Ronald Rolheiser says:

> To say that God does not create hell or send anyone there does not downplay the existence of evil and sin or the danger of eternal punishment; it only pinpoints their origins and makes clear who it is who makes the judgement and who it is who does the sentencing. God does neither; he neither creates hell nor sends anyone to it. We do both.

So if God doesn't abandon us, and God doesn't punish or condemn us, how does God react when we sin?

To answer this question I want to take you on an imaginary journey.

You are out with your friends one night. Your parents have told you to be home at 12:00 midnight. It is now 1:30 AM and you are still not home. It was a great night, but now you are scared about the reaction you are going to get when you get home. On the way home what do you do? You do what is natural: you rehearse your story. You rehearse the story you are going to tell! You lost track of time. The bus didn't come. The cab was late. You choose and learn your story by heart. Then you arrive home. The house is in darkness. You are hopeful that everybody is in bed asleep. You very quietly approach the door and slowly put the key in the lock. You open the door in silence. You step into the house. You close the door behind you. You don't put on the light. You very carefully put your foot on the first stair. You breathe a little easier thinking that you have gotten away with it. Then it happens. The disembodied voice comes from the room, "What time do you call this?" You are caught, and you have to face the music!

Now, I want you to think about a different ending. You manage to get into the house quietly. Your foot is on the first step of the stairs, and when the voice comes, instead of yelling, "What time do you call this?" the voice says with joy, "It is wonderful to have you home. It's late but let's have a party!" How would you react?

When I talked like this to a group of young people and asked at the end how they would react one of them just said, "Father, you are crazy! That would never happen!"

Would it never happen? Jesus tells us a story in the Gospel of Luke. It is about a father who has two sons. His younger son asks his father for his inheritance immediately. This was a terrible thing to ask for because what he was, in fact, saying was, "Father, I wish you were dead. You have lived too long. I want what I would get if you were to die now." The father must have been so hurt. It is an awful thing for a son to say to his father. In the story the father gave the son exactly what he asked for. The son went away, and he lived a high life making bad choices. He spent all his money. Then the country he was in experienced a famine, and he was starving, near death. He decided that he would go home to his father because no matter how bad life would be at home, at least he wouldn't starve.

His father would at least let him eat with the animals! Like us all, he rehearsed his story on the way home.

His father did one thing all the time his son was away: he waited on his son to come home. He just waited and waited. He never gave up on his son. He never condemned him. He had every reason to do both. He could have refused to give his son anything. He could have cut him out of his will. He could have told him never to come back. He did none of these things. He just waited and waited for his son to come home. The neighbors must have thought that he was an old fool. They must have seen him out looking in vain for his son to come home. They probably laughed at him and told him to give up on the boy. But he didn't. He just waited and watched and waited.

Then the day came. Out in the distance he saw his son. What did he do? Did he go back into the house and say, "Well, he can come in here on his knees and beg for forgiveness"? Or, "I'll make that son of mine suffer"? Or, "He is getting nothing more from me"? Of course not. When the father saw his son coming, he ran out to meet him. When the son started to make the speech that he had rehearsed on the way home, the father stopped him. He needed no explanations or excuses. He just hugged him and held him and announced that he was going to have a party because his son had come home. It was a joy-filled and love-filled moment. It was a tender and forgiving moment.

This story answers clearly the question, "How does God react when we sin?" He waits and waits for us to come home, and he forgives us. He is the loving parent who waits and never gives up hope. When his child comes home, he throws a party! If this is crazy, then God is crazy! There is no punishment, no abandonment, only joy and peace. But is this fair? Is forgiveness fair?

Is forgiveness fair?

Is forgiveness fair? At many levels the answer is obviously no. It is not fair to forgive. When the father in the story hugged his son and had a party to celebrate his return home, there was one person who was not happy. That person was the older son. He had been out in the fields working and heard all the commotion, and he'd asked somebody what was going on. When he was told that his brother had come home and that his father was having a party for him, he was furious. He hadn't left home. He had remained faithful to his father. He had been his father's main support while his brother was away living the high life. Now he was supposed to join in the celebrations. It was too much to ask. It wasn't fair. The older son complained bitterly to his father. His father's response was beautiful. He said,

All I have is yours. But it was right that we celebrate because this brother of yours was dead and he is alive. He was lost and is found.

The father's forgiveness for his younger son did not affect his relationship with his older son. He trusted his older son with everything. However, he still needed to celebrate because his other son had come home. It would have been very interesting to witness the meeting of the two brothers. How did they relate to each other? The younger brother at that stage must have been overcome with gratitude and emotion because of the way his father had received him and welcomed him home. The older brother might have struggled more. He probably struggled to forgive his brother, not only for squandering half of the family estate, but also for breaking his father's heart. How could he forgive his brother? What does it actually mean to forgive another person?

Forgiveness is very difficult. Sometimes people believe that to forgive is something that you do in a moment and that is it. Nothing could be further from the truth. Forgiveness is a journey, and it is not a straightforward journey. Sometimes we are good at forgiving, and other times we are not.

Part of our resistance to forgiving can come from a belief that by forgiving the other person we are letting them off. They no longer have to pay for what they have done, and that, we feel, is not fair. And in many ways this is true. But forgiveness goes beyond revenge. One can argue that an eye for an eye is justice. But forgiveness does not look for an eye for an eye. Forgiveness acknowledges that an eye for an eye leaves everybody blind. Forgiveness goes beyond justice to a place of generosity. The one who forgives is profoundly generous.

The truth is that forgiveness frees the person who has hurt us. However, not to forgive can curtail our own freedom. Often if we cannot forgive people, we spend so much time talking about them and thinking about them that we are never free of them. They may not be aware of the hold they have over us. When we don't forgive, we can actually become a slave to those we cannot forgive. Whether they are aware of it or not, they can have a very strong hold over us. In that sense forgiveness is about letting them go. Then it is up to the people who have been forgiven to take responsibility for their wrongdoing. To have been forgiven is not an excuse for avoiding responsibility.

Jean Vanier believes that there are three stages on the difficult road to forgiveness. He says:

> Some years ago I spoke with a woman in Rwanda. Seventy-five members of her family had been killed. "I have so much hate in my heart," she said, "and everyone is talking about reconciliation!" I asked her if she wanted to kill those people who had killed her family. "No," she answered. "Too many people have been killed already!" I said to her: "Do you know that the first movement in the process of forgiveness is not to seek revenge? You are on the road to forgiveness."
>
> I heard about a woman who had been put in prison because of a man's false testimony. She did not know about Jesus but met regularly for support with a religious sister. One day she met Jesus and discovered the gospel message. It was a revelation for her. The Sister asked her if she could look at forgiving the man who had given the false testimony. "No," she replied. "He has hurt

me too much." "But," she added, "I pray for him each day, that he may be liberated from all the evil in him." The second step in the process of forgiveness is to pray for those who consciously or unconsciously have hurt us.

Another step is to become conscious of who the person is who has hurt us, how he or she came to be as they are. Where are the fears in them? How did these fears come about? They, too, have been deeply hurt somewhere. Little by little, we begin to understand them.

For one who has been very hurt this journey to forgiveness can be painful and difficult. To go from not wanting to harm them to praying for them to ultimately trying to understand them and their actions can be an incredible challenge. However, it is the road to freedom for the person who is trying to forgive.

When we refuse to forgive or feel we can't forgive, it is like trying to live life with your fists clenched all the time. The first thing is that it takes a lot of energy to keep your fists clenched. The second thing is that if you keep your fists clenched, you have, in fact, disabled yourself. There is so little you can do with clenched fists apart from punching another person. Try lifting a cup with clenched fists. Try showering! When we forgive, we open our fists. We let go and we free ourselves and, yes, the other person also.

Does forgiving mean that we are weak and don't have the courage to fight for our revenge or at least get an apology from the one who has hurt us? Is forgiveness weakness? Forgiveness is far from weakness. It is extremely courageous. Examples of people who have forgiven terrible wrongs show how heroic it is.

Immaculee Ilibagiza is from Rwanda. During the genocide of 1994 her family was brutally murdered. For ninety-one days, she and seven other women were confined to a small bathroom in a pastor's house. They were not able to make noise as they were being hunted by hundreds of people with machetes wanting to kill them. In this horrendous situation Immaculee discovered forgiveness:

> One night I heard screaming not far from
> the house, and then a baby crying. The
> killers must have slain the mother and left
> her infant to die in the road. The child wailed
> all night; by morning, its cries were feeble

and sporadic, and by nightfall, it was silent. I heard dogs snarling nearby and shivered as I thought about how that baby's life had ended. I prayed for God to receive the child's innocent soul, and then asked Him, *How can I forgive people who would do such a thing to an infant?*

I heard his answer as clearly as if we'd been sitting in the same room chatting: *You are all my children . . . and the baby is with Me now.*

It was such a simple sentence, but it was the answer to the prayers I'd been lost in for days.

The killers were like children. Yes, they were barbaric creatures who would have to be punished severely for their actions, but they were still children. They were cruel, vicious, and dangerous, as kids sometimes can be, but nevertheless, they were children. . . . Their minds had been infected with the evil that had spread across the country, but their *souls* weren't evil. Despite their atrocities, they were children of God, and I could forgive a child, although it would not be easy . . . especially when that child was trying to kill me.

In God's eyes, the killers were part of His family, deserving of love and forgiveness. . . . At that moment, I prayed for the killers, for their sins to be forgiven. . . . I took a crucial step towards forgiving the killers that day. My anger was draining from me—I'd opened my heart to God, and He'd touched it with His infinite love. For the first time, I pitied the killers. I asked God to forgive their sins and turn their souls toward His beautiful light.

That night I prayed with a clear conscience and a clean heart. For the first time since I entered the bathroom, I slept in peace.

What Immaculee did was heroic. In many ways she was able to forgive because of the strength and insight that God gave her. Forgiveness can often be described as a gift. This is understandable. It is a gift—the gift of freedom. It is particularly a gift for the one who is forgiven. However, for the one who forgives, forgiveness is also a cross. The fact that Jesus was hanging on the cross when he said, "Father, forgive them for they know not what they do," reveals that forgiveness given is a cross. To forgive can be a very heavy burden.

Sometimes we can talk easily about forgiveness. We use a phrase like, "Forgive and forget," which actually makes little sense: it is not possible to forgive and forget unless you are afflicted with an illness of the mind that doesn't permit you to remember. It is very important not to trivialize forgiveness or to undermine the struggle that it is. It is also important not to idealize it in a self-congratulatory way as a massively praiseworthy act. We need to keep real about forgiveness, but we also need to realize that with God's help forgiveness is always possible. The fruit of forgiveness is freedom from the poison of hatred, and as Immaculee reveals, it also brings peace to the person who forgives.

All of this reveals the amazing gift that God gives us when he forgives us. He gives us the gift of freedom. He gives us the gift of peace. Like the father in the story of the two sons, God waits and waits on us to come home to him so that we can accept his gift of forgiveness. God wants to forgive us. God always wants to forgive us no matter what we have done. He doesn't want to punish us. He doesn't want to be separated from us. He wants to hug us and hold us and show us his mercy. If he sees any openness at all to receive his forgiveness, he runs to us. No matter what we have done—no matter how much we have sinned—he waits for us to accept his forgiveness.

The reality of God's forgiveness in our lives was revealed to me in a very surprising encounter. It was an encounter caused by the polar bear on the back cover of this book. I was attracted to this photograph in a market stall in Covent Garden in London. The photograph had been taken in the Arctic Circle by a photographer called Andrew Scriven. I thought it was marvelous photograph: a wonderful study of a polar bear. At the stall there were other great photographs, too. There were many of animals in the Arctic Circle and also in Africa.

He had another photograph that caught my attention, a mysterious beautiful photograph full of delicate colors, but there was nothing too defined in it. I thought that I could see sky, sea, and land. I asked Andrew where the photograph had been taken. He told me that he had taken the photograph in the Arctic Circle at midnight the previous August. So, it was a photograph taken at midnight in the Arctic Circle, in August 2014. I was fascinated by it, and the reason I was fascinated by it was the fact that there was so much color and light at midnight. I can understand that, when it is midnight here, in another part of the world it is daylight, but that is because it is not midnight in the other part of the world. What really caught my imagination here was that this photograph full of amazing light had been taken at midnight, and my only experience of midnight has been of darkness. I have never been anywhere where it is bright at midnight. I believe that that photograph, shown on the front cover of this book, and that concept of brightness at midnight reveals something to us about the forgiveness of God and ultimately about the sacrament of Reconciliation. No matter how dark aspects of our lives may be (and sin causes darkness in our lives), no matter how dark our lives are, there is always a light present in our lives at the same time. Our lives are never, ever completely dark. There is always light in our lives. The light shines in the present moment. The light is not simply a memory of happier times. The light shines now, and that light, I believe, is the light of God. And the light of God shines brightest in the gift of forgiveness.

How does God give us the gift of forgiveness?

Another way of asking this question is, how do we find the light of God shining in our lives? Where do we go to find this light—to become aware of this light? What these questions are asking is, how does God relate to us? It is God's desire to be in a deep and loving relationship with each one of us. How does God express his friendship?

One of the most powerful ways that God expresses his friendship is through the sacraments of the Church. Each of the sacraments is a gift from God to express his love for us and his desire to be in relationship with us. Jean Vanier says that the sacraments are doors through which we can enter to come closer and closer to God. This is a wonderful image. God has told us that he stands at the door of our lives and knocks. In God's life he leaves the doors wide open and just hopes that we come running in because we want to be with God.

If we enter the door of the sacrament of Baptism, we receive the gift of belonging. We belong to the body of Jesus in Baptism. If we enter the door of the sacrament of Confirmation, we receive the gift of God's confidence. God declares his confidence in us when the Holy Spirit pitches his tent in our lives. I think that it is marvelous when the sacrament of Confirmation takes place early in a child's life. It reveals that God has confidence in us from the beginning. What age are you when the state has enough confidence in you to let you vote? What age are you when your parents have enough confidence in you to trust you with their credit card? Yet God's confidence is not age dictated. God has confidence in us because he knows us better than anybody else. His confidence is well placed and celebrated in the sacrament of Confirmation.

If we enter the door of the sacrament of the Eucharist, we receive the gift of communion. When

Jesus entrusts himself to us in Holy Communion, it is not a reward for being a good person; it is so that we can go out from the Eucharist and be the presence of Jesus for others—so that we can live in Holy Communion with one another.

If we enter the door of the sacrament of Reconciliation, we receive the gift of forgiveness. When we are forgiven, we become aware that God's confidence is still with us. We become aware that we are still called to be Jesus for others and to live in Holy Communion. We become aware that we still belong in the body of Jesus—in the heart of God.

These are the gifts that we receive in the sacraments. But how does God reveal these gifts to us? What does God use to reveal these gifts? The amazing answer is that he uses very ordinary and natural and real things. To reveal the gift of belonging in Baptism, God uses water. To reveal the gift of God's confidence in Confirmation, God uses oil. To reveal the gift of Holy Communion in the Eucharist, God uses bread and wine. To reveal the gift of forgiveness in Reconciliation, God uses the priest. God always uses his creation to reveal his love and his friendship. If truth be told, most people don't question why he uses water or oil or bread and wine, but some do question the necessity of the priest in the sacrament of Reconciliation. They ask why they cannot confess their sins directly to God.

This is probably one of the most asked questions in relation to the sacrament of Reconciliation: why the priest? It can be difficult to confess our sins to another human being. What would be wrong with confessing directly to God and so cutting out the middle man? It is right that we talk to God directly. We need to do this often. Yet when God is revealing his gifts in the sacraments, we see that he uses very ordinary, natural, and real things. The priest falls into this category! Not only is the priest ordinary, natural, and real, the priest is also one who commits sins like all those he celebrates the sacrament with. The priest himself needs to go to Confession. He cannot forgive himself. He needs to confess to another priest. So why does God choose to communicate the light of his forgiveness through the priest?

A priest is an ordained leader in the community who has been given the gift from God of forgiving sins. For me to understand better why to confess to a priest, I found an answer in the book of Kings, in the Bible, where there is a story about a man called Naaman.

Naaman was a Syrian man. He had leprosy, and in his house there was a slave girl or a servant girl who was from Israel. She said to Naaman, "There is a prophet in my country who can cure you." So, Naaman went to the king and got permission to go to his servant's country, to Israel. He brought his people with him, and they went to the prophet Elisha's house. When Naaman arrived at Elisha's house, Elisha didn't come out of the house. He just sent the word to Naaman to go and dip in the river Jordan seven times and he would be cured. Naaman was furious. He said, "I am an important man. I have come all this distance. There are plenty of good rivers in my own country. Why would I go down into your river and dip and be cured? Why can I not do it in my own country?" The people with Naaman said, "Look, he didn't ask you to do too much. Just do this and you might be cured." They convinced Naaman, and he went down to the Jordan and he was cured. It took great humility for Naaman to go into that river. And it takes great humility for us to confess our sins to another human being. Yet this is what God invites us to do. Why? Only God knows.

What happens in the sacrament?

When this question is answered, it might do away with a lot of the fear that can be associated with the sacrament. When I asked the Youth Team for their questions about the sacrament, the first question they asked was, "Why is it so scary?" It is true that some people do find the sacrament very scary. One of the reasons for this is that stories abound about how priests became very angry during the sacrament. Some of these stories are fiction, but unfortunately many of them are real. Pope Francis, when he was speaking to priests, talked about two different kinds of priests who hear Confessions—the rigorist and the laxist. Pope Francis says,

The rigorist washes his hands of them:
in fact, he nails the person to the law,
understood in a cold and rigid way; and
the laxist also washes his hands of them:
he is only apparently merciful, but in reality
he does not take seriously the problems
of that conscience, by minimizing the sin.
True mercy takes the person into one's
care, listens to him attentively, approaches
the situation with respect and truth, and
accompanies him on the journey of
reconciliation. And this is demanding, yes,
certainly. The truly merciful priest behaves
like the Good Samaritan . . . but why does he
do it? Because his heart is capable of having
compassion, it is the heart of Christ!

There is no place for a lack of mercy in the priest
who is celebrating the sacrament. He is to be the
compassionate and merciful heart of Jesus. A great
example of how merciful and compassionate Jesus is
can be found in the Gospel story about the woman
who was caught committing adultery. In the story
the woman was going to be stoned in public for her
sin. Jesus stopped the process and invited those who
themselves had not sinned to stone her. Everybody

walked away. When Jesus was left alone with the woman he said,

> Woman, where are they? Has no one condemned you?

> When she responded that nobody had condemned her Jesus said,

> Neither do I condemn you, go away and don't sin any more.

Jesus showed profound mercy and compassion to this woman. He saved her life through his mercy and compassion. He did not condemn her, but perhaps the greatest moment of compassion came at the very end when he said, "Don't sin any more." Jesus was honest with her. He acknowledged that she had sinned.

Sometimes we think that the compassionate thing is to ignore the sin or trivialize it. That is at best misguided compassion. The other thing we can do is expose the sin and humiliate the woman. That is what the people who dragged the woman out into the public square wanted to do. That is not compassion either. It is just humiliation. So the priest is not called to ignore or humiliate. He is called to be the heart of Jesus. When he is the heart of Jesus, it is certainly not scary!

The other reason we may find celebrating the sacrament of Reconciliation scary is that we focus so much on ourselves in preparation for the sacrament and on our sinfulness. When that is our only focus, there is a danger that we can feel we are so bad that there is no hope that God could really forgive us. But there is no sin that God won't forgive. In the sacrament of Reconciliation, it is not all about us and our sinfulness. We are not the only ones who confess. We don't even confess first.

The primary focus in the sacrament of Reconciliation is God and God's light in our lives. The first person who confesses is God. What does God confess? God confesses his love, his trust, his forgiveness, to the one who comes to the sacrament. God confesses first, and he confesses that he loves us and he knows our whole story.

In the sacrament of Reconciliation, then, we are given a sacred space, an absolutely sacred space where we can name difficult and painful realities about our lives, and we do this in the light of God's forgiveness. In that sacred space, we hear the confession of God when he confesses that he loves us, that he trusts us, that he has confidence in us, and that he forgives us. So, it is good for us to confess.

Here, we have come to the heart of this book. The questions that the Youth Team asked me about the sacrament show that it is often seen as something based on formal laws. We seem to have developed an understanding of the sacrament as one where the focus is almost exclusively on the person who confesses. They have to go through proper rituals to get it right. This approach does not acknowledge the friendship that is being celebrated in the sacrament. It doesn't reflect the reality that God confesses his love for the sinner first; and that same God who confesses his love for the sinner is the father who waited and waited for his son to come home and then threw a party for him when he finally did.

St. Peter will help us to understand more clearly what happens in the sacrament. From the moment Peter denies Jesus until he is sent out by Jesus to feed his flock after the Resurrection, the sacrament of Reconciliation is revealed.

As I have already said, Peter is something of a disaster. He gets so many things wrong. His greatest disaster is denying Jesus in his hour of need. As we know, Peter then weeps bitterly. He doesn't weep bitterly because he has broken the law. He weeps bitterly because he has denied his friend. He has denied the person he loves.

There are four parts to the sacrament of Reconciliation. The first part is *contrition*. What is contrition? Contrition is when we are sorry for having done wrong. It is when we actually feel the hurt that we have caused. Peter was so contrite about hurting Jesus that he wept bitterly.

How do we feel when we sin? How do we feel when we hurt Jesus? How do we prepare for the sacrament of Reconciliation? Do we allow ourselves to feel the pain that our sins have caused? Often, perhaps, we don't. We can be so focused on thinking about what we are going to say to the priest that it becomes a memory exercise rather than a deep sharing between two friends. The Youth Team wanted to know what words we must use in Confession. What if one forgets one's sins? Why is Confession so formal? All of these questions are relevant, but when the context becomes the entering into the loving embrace of the father who is waiting for us, these questions may not seem as necessary. When we are going to visit someone who loves us, do we worry about what we are going to say? Do we worry that we are going to forget to say something? Are we going to be self-conscious about what we say or do? Is it a formal situation? The answer to these questions is no. Our focus is on the one who loves us. We want to talk to those who love us because we trust their love for us and we value their wisdom. If we hurt them, we need desperately to be reconciled with them again.

When our focus is on the one who loves us, we will naturally be heartbroken if we have hurt that person or created a distance between him or her and ourselves, forced him or her to wait for us to come home. The awareness makes us weep bitterly. This is pure contrition: we experience deep sorrow that we have not been faithful to the one we love. This is the spirit with which we enter the door of the sacrament of Reconciliation: a spirit of sorrow. Peter reveals this spirit to us. He reveals contrition to us. This is difficult and it is painful. The reason contrition is painful is that true contrition insists we be fully aware of the sin we have committed against the one we love. Contrition only becomes real when we take responsibility for our actions. When Peter acknowledged to himself that he had denied his friend Jesus, his reaction was to weep bitterly. His tears came because he loved Jesus. When we grow in love for Jesus, we also grow in pain for the times when we deny him. Peter's pain was immense.

In the Gospel we don't hear anything more about Peter throughout Jesus's agonizing death by crucifixion. We are told that John the apostle was at the foot of the cross of Jesus, but there is no mention of Peter. Perhaps he was afraid or ashamed and went away on his own to hide. He was probably full of guilt. There was nothing that he could do. The words he had spoken couldn't be taken back. The clock couldn't be turned back. He had denied his beloved friend. What was done was done and couldn't be undone. This must have been a very lonely time for Peter.

We know the next part of the story. Jesus was crucified; he died and was buried. Then early on the first day of the week, he rose from the dead. He had told his friends that this is what would happen, but they obviously hadn't understood him fully because they were shocked when they realized that Jesus had indeed risen from the dead.

Peter was back with the group when Jesus rose from the dead. When the women, who were the first to meet Jesus after the Resurrection, went to tell the apostles what had happened, Peter and John ran to the empty tomb. How did Peter feel, I wonder, when he realized that Jesus had risen from the dead? How did Peter feel about meeting Jesus again, having denied him?

This meeting came when the apostles were gathered in the room and Jesus appeared among them. The first thing that he did was to give them the gift of peace. He said, "Peace be with you." Then he spoke these incredible words:

As the father has sent me so am I
sending you.

Apart from John, all the apostles seem to have abandoned Jesus; we know for certain that Peter denied him. Aware of all of this, Jesus still declared his confidence in his friends by sending them out to do his work: to be his presence in the world.

What was Peter thinking in that room? He must have been in turmoil. Maybe he was standing at the back, hiding, wondering if Jesus had seen him. I am sure that he couldn't believe that Jesus would send him out—that Jesus would still have confidence in him. This was a very difficult moment for Peter. Should he stand up and confess his sin? Should he slip quietly away? How can he restore his friendship with Jesus? Peter's life must have seemed very dark in that room. Where was the light? Did the light shine only in the good times, the glory times, the times when Jesus was popular and when he, Peter, was so proud to be with him? Could Peter only find the light in his life by remembering the past?

If we stay in the moment of contrition—of deep sorrow in our lives—we can be overcome with guilt and shame, and it can become very, very dark. So what did Peter do?

We find out the next time that Peter met Jesus. The apostles were out fishing. They were about one hundred yards from the shore when they saw a person on the beach. They realized that it was Jesus. When Peter realized it was Jesus, he did what appeared to be a foolish thing. They were nearly at the shore, but Peter, in his impatience to meet Jesus, jumped out of the boat and swam and ran to the shore ahead of the others. Why does he do this? Why does Peter need to meet Jesus before the others come? He needs to confess.

This is the second part of the sacrament of Reconciliation: *confession*. It wasn't enough for Peter to weep bitterly and feel sorrow for having denied his friend; he needed to confess to Jesus what he had done. He needed to express his sorrow to Jesus. This is a human need that we all have—this need to admit to the sinfulness of our actions. We can never be happy if we don't. We can only take full responsibility for our actions when we admit to them.

Today many people spend money on therapy and counseling to help them deal with their past. When we confess our sin, we deal with the reality of the sinful parts of our past. If we want peace, we need to confess. I have no doubt that this is what Peter did. He couldn't confess publicly with the others in the room when Jesus appeared among them. He needed to do it quietly, privately. Jesus never revealed to the others what Peter had confessed.

Today, in the sacrament of Reconciliation, nothing is revealed either about what is confessed. This is called the Seal of Confession. It means that the priest is bound by absolute secrecy. He can never reveal what has been said. When we confess our sinfulness in the sacrament of Reconciliation, we do it in a safe and absolutely confidential and sacred place. In answer to the Youth Team's question, "Does the priest remember what you have said in Confession?" the answer is he probably doesn't, but even if he did, it wouldn't matter. He can never break the Seal of Confession.

Peter's confession to Jesus introduces us to the third part of the sacrament of Reconciliation: *forgiveness*. Peter has come to realize that even in the darkness of his denial of Jesus there is a light shining in his life. The light is the light of forgiveness. Jesus communicated that forgiveness, I have no doubt, by giving Peter a warm hug. The forgiveness was celebrated by their having a meal on the shore. This reminds us of what God says in the book of Revelation:

I stand at the door and knock. If anyone opens the door I will go in and have a meal with that person.

When Peter opened the door of his life to the light of forgiveness, Jesus and he celebrated their reconciliation by sharing a meal together. When we receive the forgiveness of God in the sacrament of Reconciliation, that forgiveness is celebrated when we come around the altar to receive Jesus in the Eucharist.

The moment when the priest absolves us from our sins is the moment when we accept God's forgiveness and our reconciliation with him. There are three parts to the absolution: the laying on of hands; the words of absolution; and the sign of the cross. When the priest lays his hands on us he says:

> God the Father of mercies, through the death
> and resurrection of his Son has reconciled
> the world to himself and sent the Holy
> Spirit among us for the forgiveness of sins.
> Through the ministry of the Church may God
> grant you pardon and peace. I absolve you
> from your sins in the name of the Father and
> of the Son and of the Holy Spirit. Amen.

The moment of forgiveness or absolution is not the end. There is a fourth stage to the sacrament of

Reconciliation. That stage is called satisfaction, or *penance*.

Peter and Jesus had a meal together, but there was still another stage to go. When they had finished their meal, Jesus asked Peter a very simple question:

> Do you love me?

Peter replied immediately:

> You know that I love you.

Jesus said to him:

> Feed my lambs.

Then Jesus asked Peter the same question again and Peter answered in the same way, and Jesus said again:

> Feed my lambs.

Jesus asked Peter a third time:

> Do you love me?

Peter was getting upset at Jesus's persistence and he said:

You know everything. You know I love you.

Jesus said:

Feed my sheep.

Jesus was expressing his trust in Peter to care for those Jesus himself loved. This brings us back to the amazing trust that God has in each one of us. When the light of forgiveness shines in our lives, that light has the power to change our lives. This is what penance or satisfaction is about. Sometimes people think that penance is some way of paying for one's sins. Sometimes we welcome punishment for what we do wrong. Punishment can make us feel better about having done wrong. One of the questions the Youth Team asked was, "If you have done your penance, have you paid for your sins?" However, the penance in the sacrament of Reconciliation is not about payment or punishment at all. The penance is to help us show through our actions the change that we have made in our lives as a result of having been forgiven.

The gift of forgiveness calls us to conversion. It calls us to change, to be better, to try not to sin again. This is why forgiveness is not an excuse to keep sinning. The Youth Team asked, "Does this sacrament condone sinning or 'being bad' because you will always be offered forgiveness?" We accept the gift of forgiveness when we take responsibility for what we have done. That is why we confess before we can accept forgiveness. Evidence that we have accepted responsibility can be found in our efforts to be converted—to change.

How do we change? When I was studying to be a priest we were often told that if we wanted to be good priests, we had to change. At one level I could understand this, and at another level it confused me. Was I supposed to try and change and become like somebody else? Should I pick a saint and try to copy that saint's life? Surely it is good to be inspired by other people. Surely it is good to learn from other people. But I can never be that other person. The father of a friend of mine, a businessman, was giving a speech at a graduation ceremony. He said:

> Be yourself at all times. Be your own role
> model. If you try to be someone else you will
> never be authentic. But no one can beat you
> at being yourself.

So if you are to remain as yourself, how do you change? This is where my confusion lay. However, when we think again about that sacred sanctuary within us—that fair land, the place of our conscience—the place where God lives, the confusion disappears. When we are called and given the power to change, it is not to be somebody else or even to mimic somebody else. We are called to become more and more ourselves. I am called to be the person that God created, not the person I think I would like to be or the person I think others would like me to be. I am called to be absolutely and completely me! When I become fully myself, then I am at home down in that fair land of my life with God. When I am at home there, I cannot sin. I am united with God.

The penance that we receive in the sacrament of Reconciliation helps us to be at home down there in our conscience with God. The "penance" that Peter received was to care for those Jesus loved. It is when

we care for others that we become fully ourselves.
Jean Vanier says,

> But Peter can only guide, nourish and be
> responsible for people
> in the name of Jesus *if he loves Jesus,*
> and I dare say *if he loves Jesus passionately*
> and is prepared to give his life for Jesus.
> We can only assume a responsibility in the
>   name of Jesus
> if we love Jesus and become his friend.
> This is not something devotional or sentimental.
> It is a commitment to help people
> to whom we are not especially attracted
> to grow in their love of Jesus
> and to work with them.
> Not seeking to control them but to liberate them.

How we treat others reveals our conversion.
How we treat others reveals how much we love
Jesus. When we receive penance in the sacrament
of Reconciliation, it is to help us to love others
more and more in the name of Jesus. This is the
real way that we spread the Good News of Jesus.
We don't do this by being defensive or by fighting
or arguing. We do it by being gentle and tender.

Gentleness and *tenderness* are not words that are used too often in society today. In many ways they can be misinterpreted as evidence of weakness. Gentleness and tenderness don't work too well if our aim is to climb up the pyramid of success. If our aim is competition and winning, we must leave our tenderness to one side. Gentleness and tenderness only enable the building up of the body of Christ. Patrick Mathias, a psychiatrist, was asked to identify an indicator of human maturity, and he answered, "tenderness." He describes tenderness as

> a sensitive opening to and respectful participation in the life of the other.

When we change and become who we really are, we joyfully and positively share the bread of the other. We share in the life of the other. Together we live in holy communion devoid of competition. Penance helps us to do this so that we can participate fully in the Eucharist, and continue to be the hands, the feet, the eyes, and the body of Jesus in the world today.

So when
and how
should we celebrate
the gift of this
sacrament that
allows us to live
in the light of
God's forgiveness?

It's a gift, and we love to receive a gift! When we become technical about how often we need to "go to Confession," we can lose sight of the gift and of the one who confesses first.

How often do you want to stand in the loving embrace of God? I would say the answer to this question is pretty often! We need to accept the gift of forgiveness when we have denied or betrayed

Jesus. We need to accept the gift of forgiveness when we behave as if we are God in our own lives. We need to accept the gift of forgiveness when we refuse to make space for Jesus in our lives.

It is also wonderful to celebrate the sacrament of Reconciliation before major events in the year and in our lives. Before Easter, before Christmas, before our birthday, before our graduation, it is so good to hear God's confession of love and forgiveness so that we are at home with God in our conscience.

When we celebrate the sacrament, it is important not to rush in and rush out. Plan for the day you are celebrating the sacrament. Make time. Maybe arrange to go with family or friends. Pray together before. Go for a walk before. After go for ice cream or coffee and donuts! Each time we celebrate the sacrament, it is a very important moment in our lives and we should try not to underestimate that.

In preparation for the celebration of the sacrament, make the journey to your place of conscience. From that place where you are united with God, examine your life since the last time you celebrated the sacrament. Think about what you did and what you didn't do in your relationship with Jesus and in your relationship with Jesus alive in other people. You can ask yourself simple questions.

> When did I behave as if I was God in my life?
> When did I refuse to make space for Jesus in my life?

One of the ways I like to examine my life is by looking at a picture! The picture is of the second station of the cross in Lourdes, France.

I think the whole world is on the road to Calvary. Everybody is there. Soldiers, crowds, Veronicas, Simons, Judases, Peters, Marys—everybody is there. The question we need to ask is, where are we? Where are we in this drama of Good Friday? We can be like the crowd and shout, "Crucify him!" We can be like Veronica and show Jesus tenderness. We can be like Judas and betray Jesus. We can be like so many of the people in the story, but where are we?

There are only two places we can be. We can be in Jesus in the body of Christ or we can be the cross. On the road to Calvary we can only be either Jesus or the cross. Our call is to be Jesus. God desires that we be the presence of his Son on the road to Calvary. God trusts us to be the presence of his Son. If we are not the presence of his Son, if we are not Jesus, then we are the cross that he carries.

The stations of the cross on the hill behind the grotto in Lourdes are so dramatic. The second station depicting Jesus receiving his cross is breathtaking. It is breathtaking because Jesus is reaching up to accept the cross. It is as if he desires to carry the cross. He has opened his hands to receive it. What is he receiving—reaching up to accept? It is this instrument of his death that will cause him to fall because of its weight. Why would he reach up to accept that and not try to avoid it—to hide away from it?

The reason that he accepts it so willingly—the reason he reaches out for it—is that the cross is a symbol of us in our sinfulness. When we sin—when we refuse to be the presence of Jesus, when we try to be God—we are part of the cross that Jesus carries to Calvary. We are part of the cross that he is nailed to. Then, when we are forgiven—when we are reconciled with Jesus in his body the Church—we become his presence. We become his love and his compassion—his tenderness and his forgiveness for others.

I examine my life by looking at the picture at the end of every day and before going to celebrate the sacrament of Reconciliation by simply asking myself, when was I the cross of Jesus and when was I the presence of Jesus?

God wants us to hear his confession of love and forgiveness in the sacrament of Reconciliation. He has humbly chosen to depend on us and to need us to be the presence of Jesus in the world. We become the presence of Jesus when we confess our need for God because we have sinned, and we accept the forgiveness of God because he always believes in us and trusts us.

In a world where we are told that positions and possessions are what matter, in the sacrament of Reconciliation God reveals what really matters. We are beautiful. He loves us. He never wants to be separated from us. He will always wait on us to come home, and when we do he will have a party. Just like the light shining in the Arctic Circle at midnight in August, at all times and in every moment of our lives the light of God's forgiveness is shining. It might take a polar bear to stop us in our tracks to remind us, but whatever it takes, find the light in your life.

Celebrate the sacrament of Reconciliation often, and become the person God created you to be.

Acknowledgments

Thank you to Jon Sweeney at Paraclete Press for asking me to write this short book. Thank you to my friend Andrew Scriven for allowing me to use his photographs on the cover of this book. Thank you to those who helped me in any way to write this book, especially my colleagues in the Derry Diocesan Catechetical Centre and the members of the Derry Youth Community.

Notes

p. 7. *Hell had the first place in her heart.*
Frank O'Connor, "My First Confession," https://www2
.bc.edu/john-g-boylan/files/first-confession.pdf
(accessed June 12, 2015).

p. 9. *Confession should not be "torture," . . .*
Pope Francis, March 12, 2015 https://w2.vatican.va/
content/francesco/en/speeches/2015/march/documents/
papa-francesco_20150312_tribunale-penitenzieria
-apostolica.html (accessed June 12, 2015).

p. 13. *With heaven my throne . . .*
Isaiah 66:1–2.

p. 18. *There must be no competition among you.*
Philippians 2:3.

p. 19. *Always consider the other person to be better than yourself . . .*
Philippians 2:3–5.

p. 21. *These months of illness . . .*
Maria Boulding OSB, *Gateway to Resurrection* (London:
Burns & Oates, 2010), 3–4.

p. 23. *Do not be afraid, I have redeemed you.*
Isaiah 43:1– 4.

p. 27. *How beautiful you are, my love . . .*
Song of Songs 1:16.

p. 27. *See where he stands behind the wall.*
Song of Songs 2:9.

p. 28. *Come then, my love . . .*
Song of Songs 2:13–14.

p. 29. *no flood can quench . . .*
Song of Songs 8:7.

p. 29. *Draw me in your footsteps.*
Song of Songs 1:4.

p. 33. *Conscience is the most secret core . . .*
Second Vatican Council, *Gaudium et Spes* (Dublin: Dominican, 1977), no. 16.

p. 33. *I regained contact with myself . . .*
Patrick Woodhouse, *Etty Hillesum: A Life Transformed* (London: Continuum, 2009), 39.

p. 34. *The inside of you is like a well . . .*
Walter Macken, *Seek the Fair Land* (London: Pan Books, 1962), 299.

p. 35. *Certainly, if I am obliged to bring religion . . .*
John Henry Newman, Letter to the Duke of Norfolk.

p. 35. *Man has the right to act in conscience . . .*
Catechism of the Catholic Church, 1782.

p. 38. *After Pentecost the apostles spoke the language of Jesus . . .*
See Acts 2:1–13.

p. 43. *Peter was the apostle whom Jesus chose to be the rock . . .*
See Matthew 16:18.

p. 43. *Get behind me, Satan!*
See Matthew 16:23.

p. 43. *When Jesus invited Peter to walk on the water to meet him . . .*
See Matthew 14:22–33.

p. 44. *Peter objected.*
See John 13:1–17.

p. 44. *Peter would deny him three times.*
See John 13:38.

p. 44. *his reaction was to weep bitterly.*
See Matthew 26:75.

p. 46. *I stand at the door and knock.*
Revelation 3:20.

p. 46. *I have come so that you may have life . . .*
John 10:10.

p. 47. *Perhaps the Ten Commandments are a road map to freedom.*
See Exodus 20:1–17.

p. 51. *we can look at the temptation of the Jesus in the desert by the devil.*
See Luke 4:1–13.

p. 55. *You must love the Lord your God with all your heart* . . .
Matthew 22:37–39.

p. 56. *On the day you eat it your eyes will be opened* . . .
Genesis 3:5.

p. 56. *I was afraid because I was naked* . . .
Genesis 3:10.

p. 60. *The innkeeper said he had no space for Joseph and his wife.*
See Luke 2:8.

p. 61. *Whatever you do to the least you do to me.*
Matthew 25:40.

p. 62. *Just as the human body* . . .
1 Corinthians 12:12–21.

p. 63. *What is more, it is precisely the part of the body* . . .
1 Corinthians 12:21–26.

p. 64. *When you give a lunch or a dinner* . . .
Luke 14:12–14.

p. 69. *Do not be afraid. I have redeemed you.*
Isaiah 43:1.

p. 70. *Does a woman forget her baby* . . .
Isaiah 49:15–16.

p. 71. *For God sent his Son into the world not to condemn the world* . . .
John 3:17–19.

p. 72. *To say that God does not create hell or send anyone there* . . .
Ronald Rolheiser, "God Judges No One," *The Catholic Herald* (September 25, 2009).

p. 74. *Jesus tells us a story in the Gospel of Luke.*
See Luke 15:11–32.

p. 78. *All I have is yours.*
Luke 15:31.

p. 80. *Some years ago I spoke with a woman in Rwanda. . . . we begin to understand them.*
Jean Vanier, *Drawn into the Mystery of Jesus Through the Gospel of John* (London: Darton Longman Todd, 2004), 152–53.

p. 82. *One night I heard screaming not far from the house . . .*
Immaculee Ilibagiza, *Left to Tell* (California: Hay House, 2006), 118–119.

p. 88. *Jean Vanier says that the sacraments are doors . . .*
Vanier, *Drawn into the mystery of Jesus through the gospel of John*, 129.

p. 92. *there is a story about a man called Naaman.*
See 1 Kings 5:1–14.

p. 94. *The rigorist washes his hands of them . . .*
Pope Francis, March 6, 2014 https://w2.vatican.va/content/francesco/en/speeches/2014/march/documents/papa-francesco_20140306_clero-diocesi-roma.html (accessed June 30, 2015).

p. 94. *the Gospel story about the woman who was caught committing adultery.*
See John 8:1–11.

p. 101. *As the father has sent me so am I sending you.*
John 20:21.

p. 103. *Peter . . . jumped out of the boat and swam and ran to the shore ahead of the others.*
See John 21:7.

p. 104. *I stand at the door and knock.*
Revelation 3:20.

p. 106. *Peter and Jesus had a meal together . . .*
See John 21:15–17.

p. 110. *But Peter can only guide, nourish and be responsible for people . . .*
Vanier, *Drawn into the Mystery of Jesus Through the Gospel of John*, 353.

About Paraclete Press

Who We Are

Paraclete Press is a publisher of books, recordings, and DVDs on Christian spirituality. Our publishing represents a full expression of Christian belief and practice—from Catholic to Evangelical, from Protestant to Orthodox.

We are the publishing arm of the Community of Jesus, an ecumenical monastic community in the Benedictine tradition. As such, we are uniquely positioned in the marketplace without connection to a large corporation and with informal relationships to many branches and denominations of faith.

What We Are Doing

Paraclete Press Books Paraclete publishes books that show the richness and depth of what it means to be Christian. Although Benedictine spirituality is at the heart of all that we do, we publish books that reflect the Christian experience across many cultures, time periods, and houses of worship. We publish books that nourish the vibrant life of the church and its people.

We have several different series, including the best-selling Paraclete Essentials and Paraclete Giants series of classic texts in contemporary English; Voices from the Monastery—men and women monastics writing about living a spiritual life today; award-winning poetry; best-selling gift books for children on the occasions of baptism and first communion; and the Active Prayer Series that brings creativity and liveliness to any life of prayer.

Mount Tabor Books Paraclete's newest series, Mount Tabor Books, focuses on liturgical worship, art and art history, ecumenism, and the first millennium church, and was created in conjunction with the Mount Tabor Ecumenical Centre for Art and Spirituality in Barga, Italy.

Paraclete Recordings From Gregorian chant to contemporary American choral works, our recordings celebrate the best of sacred choral music composed through the centuries that create a space for heaven and earth to intersect. Paraclete Recordings is the record label representing the internationally acclaimed choir Gloriæ Dei Cantores, praised for their "rapt and fathomless spiritual intensity" by *American Record Guide*; the Gloriæ Dei Cantores Schola, specializing in the study and performance of Gregorian chant; and the other instrumental artists of the Gloriæ Dei Artes Foundation.

Paraclete Press is also privileged to be the exclusive North American distributor of the recordings of the Monastic Choir of St. Peter's Abbey in Solesmes, France, long considered to be a leading authority on Gregorian chant.

Paraclete Video Our DVDs offer spiritual help, healing, and biblical guidance for a broad range of life issues including grief and loss, marriage, forgiveness, facing death, bullying, addictions, Alzheimer's, and spiritual formation.

Learn more about us
at our website
www.paracletepress.com
or phone us toll-free at
1.800.451.5006

SCAN
TO
READ
MORE

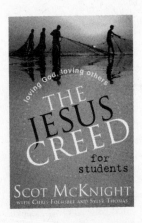

The Jesus Creed for Students
Loving God, Loving Others

Scot McKnight

ISBN: 978-1-55725-883-0, $13.99, Paperback

New Testament scholar McKnight shows how this double commandment to love makes sense and gives shape to the moral lives of young adults. *The Jesus Creed for Students* aims to demonstrate a simple truth—that followers of Jesus, follow Jesus. (Also, it's practical, filled with stories, and backed up and checked by youth pastors.)

AND FOR YOUR PARENTS:

Freedom and Forgiveness
A Fresh Look at the Sacrament of Reconciliation

Father Paul Farren

ISBN: 978-1-61261-498-4, $8.99, Paperback

"**F**ather Paul's new book is a beautiful invitation into the sacrament of Reconciliation, perhaps the most misunderstood sacrament in the church. With his clear, helpful, and accessible writing, *Freedom and Forgiveness* reminds the reader that the sacrament is about not how bad you are, but how good God is."

—James Martin, SJ, author of *Jesus: A Pilgrimage*